Elaine Beckett

Sea Creature
Regrows Entire Body

VERVE
POETRY PRESS
BIRMINGHAM

PUBLISHED BY VERVE POETRY PRESS
https://vervepoetrypress.com
mail@vervepoetrypress.com

FIRST PUBLISHED APR 2021

Printed and bound in the UK
by Imprint Digital, Exeter

ISBN: 978-1-912565-57-3

For Gillian Barr

CONTENTS

Sea Creature Regrows Entire Body

Thursday

When the dusk comes in as quiet as this
as low as this, as dense as this,
like your whole world has gone back to where it began
and you wonder how you got into this mess,
the kind of mess you cannot see an end to
as if it may already have ended very badly
and all you can hear is the sound of your own name
spoken deep inside your own head,
it is probably best to step back
from whatever kind of brink you imagine
you have reached
and think about something else,
something small and practical
like boiling an egg.

To Leave You Now

is to leave these petals at your door
for all the facts we might have spilled
concerning damage;

your news impossible to hide,
mine impossible to share
for all the shame that might ensue

so I kept quiet, and so did you,
knowing that to name such things
would grant them irretrievable reality.

I love the way we skirt around such topics
as might teeter on the edge of private hell,
never penetrate each other's shell,

hope that better things may happen,
and probably will.

Sea Creature Regrows Entire Body

was the headline that stopped me short.
It took a day or two to get back to it
what with all the broken cups.

The weather was fine,
the kind of weather that makes a difference to people
who prefer not to calm down

but react to whatever the next thing is
that they think they ought to manage.
Because you don't get to decide most things,

they happen through some other force
that in a moment of distraction,
you yourself set in motion:

the brushing of a tiny hair,
the turning of the wrong key in the wrong lock
with all its transparency of knock-on effects

hours, days, even decades later
like why on earth did you marry the person
if you didn't even like them?

Of course June wasn't all like that.
Some days were sublime –
freshly milled pepper

and salt and ice-cream
and everything I've ever wanted
for the rest of my life.

American People

from an interview with the artist Faith Ringgold

I knew I had to tell it like I saw it
she said,
create images of important aspects
of American life
that affected
me.
American people,
that was the story I was going to tell.

Take Natalie:
a real beauty in her youth,
coal black with long tight braids,
they say she ran a bad house for white men,
a real successful kind of house.

It was difficult
you see,
there were riots in the streets,
all kinds of stuff happening

so when the King had his dream
I decided to weave it through all of my works:
American people sitting down together
at the table of brotherhood.

Back then they didn't show no interest
in my images
you see,
racism was everywhere, people killing each other,
all kinds of stuff.

A silence opened up:

how would she paint America now?
the interviewer asked:

I would paint it
she said,
I would paint it in multi-multi-*multi* colours
the way I did before,
only *this* time
I'd make them more obvious.

Stupor

I search for a table
in this little café town,
restless to read
what has happened
since I last heard the news.
Shadows of anger and fear
darken the already low-pressure day.
Behind the bar
a waiter talks about his acne,
how much it hurts.
I flip the page over again:

correspondents strive
to describe
yet another hellish circumstance
we've somehow condoned
through inertia, denial,
cowardice is such an old-
fashioned word these days;
these children
with their scalding throats,
whole families
in frantic suffocation.

All that we know can happen
is happening again –
I sit here, you walk there,
is there no way forward,
not one that can lead
towards hope?
You tell me there's a problem
with the car, I tell you
that I bought new soap.
We talk about grief,
about stupor.

Democracy is Coming

i.m.: Leonard Cohen, who died on the eve of Trump's election

Trucks deliver railings to a tower on 5th Avenue,
I try to write about a tree

because I heard that part of you died last night
if there is such a thing as a soul,

and fifty four men have been strung up on pylons,
fifty four souls if there is such a thing as a soul

take them with you if you can,
to wherever you might or you might not be going

in the pocket of your song that a lot of us are singing,
wrapped up safe in your old velvet jacket

if souls can be carried in the pocket of a jacket
in the pocket of a song,

I cannot write about a tree.

Other Country

for John Sopel

You wander into the other country
with its opposite conversation.

Accents don't match,
names you've never heard before

what are you – twelve?

and the pace at which things happen there,
it never stops.

You cast about for some way out of the mess.
There is no precedent.

Dropping Shoe

We cannot look and yet we do
the bundling up the dropping shoe

sky so thick we gasp and stare
he plumps for sleep she twists her chair

the satchel straps the dark red pools
their agonising dash for school

limbs so limp we gasp and stare
he'll plump for death she'll twist her hair

there's nothing nothing can be done
let's mute the sound don't watch them run

the satchel straps the dark red pools
their agonising dash from school

he'll pump for death she'll tear her hair
their skin's so white they'll gasp for air

o bundle up that pretty shoe
we cannot look and yet we do.

Calais, or Part of me is at the Opera

A boy dares to leap,
higher than expected with no hand-holds,

the roar of a truck drowning the crack
of the crush of his leg against steel

while I sit watching Carmen.
She has a lot to do:

breathing in, and breathing deep
to last this phrase

and the next, and the one after that,
pitching on towards the final act.

It is breath that we all have in common.
The boy has a life to live,

given all of it again
he still would not have chosen death.

Her Way with Avocados

was not his way.
She liked to split them round their middle
as with a circular saw,
leaving the problem of the seed to solve
then excavate one half and leave the other
somewhere unlikely;
next to the tap, half-way off a saucer
behind the kettle
to go black.

Depending on the place they were at
he found this:
dull, stubborn, idiosyncratic,
lackadaisical, disrespectful of the fruit,
foot-loose,
endearing, funny, idiotic,
ignorant of all things culinary,
obtuse.

Then one afternoon
a miracle:
months of wrestling with these pears
and other people might be right –
it might be *easier* to halve them vertically,
stalk to tip once they are ripe.
Moreover,
her precarious placing of two half-spooned skins
on top of a banana in the fruit bowl
had Miro-type experimental qualities,
which he liked.

Rehearsal for a Night-time Scene
with Thunder

Wake up slow, reach for a hand.
It won't be there.

Try to fathom who you are, and why,
then leave the bed,

pad across the room,
negotiate the eight foot six TV (in the shape of a guitar)

now try to part the drapes, they'll smell of money,
place your palms on the cool glass,

search the vertical drop,
the wet dazzle;

a curve in the curtain on your left –
it will shift a moment,

the moment you begin to make him out;
naked but for headphones and a mic,

your semi-jaded-angel-engineer,
gesturing you must not make a sound –

now wait real still while he records his track:
rain plunges eleven floors down to patched-up tarmac.

Zabriskie Point

Tomorrow I will stay in bed all day
while you my love can either choose to put
this car away or drive it to your own
untimely death along these terrifying roads.
You scream with laughter at a sign
that warns of falling rocks yet to mention
anything about your driving
would risk all that we have so far put aside,
managed to avoid on this trip
that's eating up our money like a lucky chip.
Should I offer your arm a gentle squeeze,
suggest we take a break, demand you rest?
here comes a bend with a vertical drop
on the left by a rock, and a barrier
that looks too thin, and this gigantic truck
curving our way with a toot-waving arc.
You smile at me yelling *isn't this fun!*
reach for my hand with the hand that
really should be on the steering wheel for
drivers need to grip their wheels in unfamiliar
countries driving unfamiliar cars
there'd be no-one to help us – the radio
would still be blaring whatever this is
in a major key – engine crushed, glass, guts, sun
setting blood-red across a bruised purple sky
you say the Golden Gate was narrower
than expected, ask if I'd imagined it that way;

not really I say, not with the sky as black as that
and my new swimsuit as yet unpacked,
it just popped out like that – barbed,
sixty miles before you left the highway,
drove on and on until this sign for PIES
appeared. It is good you have stopped
by a cactus tree. Perhaps to think what to say.
Will it be; this holiday's supposed to be
for us, not this car, that bin over there
or the weather – *us*, in California, together?

Instructions

What you will need more than anything
is devotion.

So the things that you find yourself doing
will not seem perverse,

at least not at the time.
Make sure you know where the pharmacy is

because you may run out. It isn't fancy dress
so wear whatever,

and remember;
you are doing this for him

not for yourself.
Switch off all the phones, including his,

and make sure you know how to
lock the front door.

To be disturbed would be the worst thing ever
and take something to eat –

you never know how long it all might last.

Two Figures on a Bridge

have chosen a background of shadowy fretwork
to rest for a while,
the way some people do when managing the heat;
his tailored shirt, her chic black hat and pristine skirt
at ease in the narrow streets.

I watch from below a flight of ragged steps
that lead down to an undercroft,
decide to take a photograph,
miss the second or two
that I thought it would take them to kiss.

They remain very still,
leaning back against opposing balustrades
facing one another.
Eventually, she tilts her head. He takes out his phone,
she takes out hers and in this amber light
they seem a perfect couple;
content to wait for each other's communications
while poised for some theatrical exchange.

I imagine it will be in Italian.
A dip in the hum of an air-conditioning box
resting high upon a window ledge seems curiously apt;
quietly getting on with itself, while several blocks
away, beyond the lap of these impenetrable waterways,
the afternoon begins: water-taxis surge to the lagoon,
thousands try to think how it would be
if no-one else were here.

I re-adjust my lens:
he's deep in whispered conversation now
while she breathes in, provides herself with small
distractions and I think; I used to have all this,
this long knowledge of another.

An older man arrives.
She moves her leg, admires her heel
then shifts her hip – I click.
It is hot. Too hot to be feeling a fool,
imagining love where no such love exists.

Sometimes

she'd ask questions that led him
to invent things

that he'd have to remember
to refer to, later on.

He made sure that he did,
like where he had been

though he hadn't been there
at least not on those days.

Sometimes he'd take a packed
lunch,

as if he were going for a long day's ride,
then cycle to the station,

catch the fast train into town
as if they'd never sold their flats,

never bought a house
at the edge of a playground

at the edge of a field,
never lost a baby.

Towards the end
the lies got so complex

that he could not remember
what he had said,

or where he was supposed
to have gone.

When he felt like that
he'd accuse her of being a slut.

A Mess of Strangers

You don't need to know about the fifty minute ride
with a driver who poured his heart out about Bach,
      one partita in particular,

leaning back to give me his phone so I could watch
a clip of him practising the piece in Stepney
      while he turned on to the Euston road.

I thought is he having me on, is this one of those key-
boards that automatically plays partitas?
      Soon I'll be feeling claustrophobic

in a stationary vehicle in an underpass, while Glen here
goes on and on about the crash that just happened
      on the M25 with this music

that's perfectly suited to both topics, though
because I'm on my way to a difficult encounter with
      a woman I have never met before,

about to entrust her with a lifetime's secret,
it is actually good that I'm watching this stranger
      play a partita I hardly ever play

while he drives me to a street I've never been to before.
Far harder to have had to worry
      about the reason I am going there

in a silent taxi, or worse still, a cab in which the only
thing to listen to would be this news about a lorry
      crossing a central reservation.

Certificate

I'd been waiting in the lobby
with its information sheets
and sign for emergency exit.

When she called me in
she didn't have
an expression on her face.

She didn't have a face at all
or any kind of clothes or legs
or any kind of hairstyle.

The only thing I needed her to have
was a functioning hand
to pass me the piece of paper

that would alter my life.
And though I'd been warned,
I didn't expect it to feel

as difficult as that: like being
taken to the Chamber of Horrors
aged six, when I'd said

I didn't want to go and see
how people got bricked up,
and after lunch, being made

to watch Bambi's mother get
shot in a strange dark cinema,
as if I were tough enough

to manage my imagination,
instead of crying like that
all the way back to the station.

Kitty and Frank

From these small fragments posted on the web
I've learned you called her *Kitty*,
that she called you *Frank*

and had sailed to New York and back
by the time she met you, at twenty two,
Third Class across the Atlantic,

as for your father's father,
I've learned he was whipped for climbing a tree
on Disraeli's estate – by Disraeli –

and Kitty and you had been years in service
when war was declared so you joined up quick,
got as far away as you possibly could

from the starch and the sweat and the labour.
It didn't turn out good,
though you put on the bravest of faces:

Dearest Kitty,

Just a note to say I am well, have been in the line six days
this last time, up to my knees in mud, feet very numb
though I managed to stick it until our time was up.
I walked out by myself. It was terrible up there.

Your loving husband,

Frank.

After the War

It was often to do with the way that he took off his belt,
laid it down carefully by that photograph
of a place he would like to have visited.

A house where, if you were a guest,
there'd likely be a towel embossed with your name
as if the owners had waited many years
for your arrival,

and on the parterre a pony with a brushed white coat
would be led past a window by a sturdy little girl,
and in the evening another of the daughters would
show off her ebony castanets,

and the house would be still enough
to cast your mind back
over what had just happened, try to make sense of it.

Falling

If I were to tell you
I know very little about myself,
you might turn away.

I'd have to move the conversation on
to something less personal, because
if I were to tell you

I met my mother for just one afternoon
I'd maybe lose confidence,
you might turn away,

see me differently,
and that would be a shame.
If I were to tell you

that shame is exactly what I felt that day
you might think me too complex, too fragile,
you might turn away.

You don't need to know everything
all at once, though I'm bursting to tell you,
if I were to tell you –
would you turn away?

Doll

Think of a doll resting in a box, waiting to be unwrapped
one special day:
coat neatly folded over dress, legs bent straight,
arms by her side so as to fit.

Muffled squeals as the box tilts up and down,
her fine brown hair pushing into
and out of her crinkled paper, a scratch of something
pressing from above;

up and down she goes again then a quick tug-yank
and the first layer's off,
tilted, then suddenly shaken so hard that she lifts right up
and lands and lifts

and bangs her face on the ceiling of the lid, shaken again
then dropped as a doorbell rings.
She has one word.
She won't say it until the stud that is stuck in her back's

pulled out. Thud of footsteps bearing down,
squeak of tiny scissors then a bark to make you jump
the living daylights – if it were you or me
by now we'd be thinking *back off*

bit stuffy yes, knees uncomfortable yes, rock-a-bye lashes
flicking too fast,
all our clothes still done up – but no, it isn't you or me
and the doll is still stuck in the box with

a worsening scrabble of tugging that's louder
and fiercer as final last layer's
ripped-off, torn
and now everyone wants to get into her space

and suddenly she's out:
born into the white-hot room with its fairy lights,
its tinsel tree, its squabble of hands
and something called a family.

Baby Shawl

Under tissue paper at the back of a drawer

    soft as air and pocketed
    with a ribbon threaded through

to have known who knitted it

    threaded the ribbon
    gathered the silk for its pocketing

in winter   because it would have been winter

to have known who folded it around tucked it inside

    soft as air and pocketed
    to keep in the warmth

though it may have been bought

    one with a creamy ribbon please
    threaded through   soft as air and pocketed

for spring   for it would have been spring

    if she sent it on afterwards

       by post.

Tortoise

Onto the gravel drive
he hauled,

ridding the smell of polish
from his claws,

edging past the privet,
the rhododendron towers,

the dripping, battered
petals,

past the Dalmatians
at number six,

keeping his head
well tucked-in,

how I envied his shell,
his tough little legs,

the scraggy neck
he could pull straight back,

on and on
to the end of the lane

where beech trees gave way
to a view,

and daffodil leaves
had been left

to rot down,
naturally.

Green Suitcase

It wasn't packed with souvenirs
only importances:
certificates for life and death
and squeezed down inside
the remains of a glove.

By the time she came back it was gone,
people pushing past, trying to get off
and she must be off
though she's searching everywhere
even the platform –

train pulling away – searching a house now
as if it were hers,
though the glistening fog seems to
question a ruse that she'd borrowed it once
from her mother

with its dark green silk and loose pockets
that had lost their elastic.
Back in the department store
she tries to insist that
all of her names are written down

with a pen that doesn't work
anymore,
and that is the way of some dreams:
they leave you entwined in the threads
of your own unconscious.

Appoggiatura

The essential nature of appoggiatura
        is its leaning quality.

Sometimes it
        leans on a dissonance.

If a grace note is added it should be crushed
        before the beat.

It calms me to read of such things.

For example;
        you can weaken a melody

through excessive use of appoggiatura
        and Quantz recommends

changing the bow.

        I do not play the violin.

Appoggiaturas gain weight and strength from
        leaning on dissonances.

Long dissonant appoggiaturas are said to be
        appuyé so I am free to read about them

entirely devoid of pressure,
        so long as they apply to the violin.

The fact that I've hardly touched the piano
        since lockdown began

is like a rule that should
        not be applied to music because

there are ways of approaching many pairs of falling
        notes that avoid misunderstanding

(I am getting all this from the book that belongs to my friend)
        and when appoggiaturas appear between notes,

a third apart, they are played unaccented and lightly slurred
onto the note that follows.

Mozart wrote that the short appoggiatura should be played
        quickly in order not to rob a piece of its liveliness

(I have tried to give it back to her on several occasions)
        and when Bach wrote the small sign

for the ornament he often preferred it to be played short
        (including today when she brought her own coffee

to drink in my garden).
        We did not talk about ornamentation,

the youth orchestra that's about to close
        or his sonata in F we'd been due to perform in July.

Afterwards I found the book again – *Baroque String Playing*
        for Ingenious Learners – here on this table,

        the one she'd preferred not to touch.

Draft Email

While you sat snug under a chandelier, inviting us
to gaze past you into a salon fit for a king – the kind of
king you imagined you would be until this *devilish disease*
came along – we were searching for elastic bands,
measuring the distance from our noses to our chins.
I wonder how you got to a place where making masks
from old T-shirts seemed an adequate instruction
from the leader of a *world-beating economy?*
Your terrible pretence at making progress always
starts with *let me be clear.*
No, let me be clear: apparently that Sunday we were not
at level 4, or at level 3, but *transitioning* from 4 to 3;
exactly where you said we were 2 weeks ago,
when you told us that you could not lift the lockdown
– then you did.
You are out of your depth; waiting for the sun to rise
in jest while lonely saturn orbits the sky and Monday
is not Monday anymore but Wednesday:
a day that you told us would go very well
so long as we kept *alert!*
And now that we can drive ourselves to death while you
get your hair cut again in a vain attempt to look sober
(before your next vacuous oration on the subject of;
why I'm not the fool you think I am)
you seem even more like a sieve, through which
all reason drains, however hard you try to
clench your fists, threaten to punch the living
daylights out of anyone bold enough
to bring you to account.

That's it for now,

stay safe.

Dear Joni

'It's clouds' illusions I recall...' - Joni Mitchell

Bring me my moccasins, my long lilac skirt,
my hand-sewn blouses embroidered at the neck,
my velvet remnants, my treadle machine,
all my Dohnányi with everything ahead of me

sky high,

in the middle of nowhere, and let it be June.

Bring me that river of loosening hair,
our long pointy collars and washed-cotton waistcoats,
set aside the recipes for total devastation
but all our purple ink, with everything ahead of us

and let there be nettles and a huge full moon

sky high,

in the middle of nowhere, in June.

Norfolk Winter '72

I'd said fuck a couple of times too many at a party
when everyone else was saying bloody

and that was it – he wanted me,
no matter I belonged to someone else.

Next day he borrowed a van, drove to the cottage
and asked for me;

stared straight at you in the firelight, under the low ceiling,
fearing you'd attack him with the poker.

Like silent stags you each compared the other's coat,
heads almost touching: how deep was the fur,

was it really from Afghanistan, had the other even
heard of Philip Roth? So of course I packed my baskets

and moved into his, any flower girl worth her candles
would have done the same.

Last Visible Dog

Horn-piano-violin combinations
have little to do with rock music.
We'd never applied ourselves to rock music,
only free improvisation
only it wasn't free,
because the violinist was anxious
about starts and finishes
so we'd have to plan ahead,
know who'd be starting each piece,
how it would finish,
making it hard to take risks in-between
which were supposed to be anyone's guess,
though we could pretty-much guess
how the music would go
as we each had our riffs that repeated,
got vaguely disguised then repeated
as if we were seriously into minimalism,
as if minimalism could disguise chaos
with which it has nothing to do.
The violinist was sure
this was the way to handle chaos.
At least it got us out of our rooms
and in my case, on the day
a silent Japanese percussionist came to play,
an extraordinary lay in Notting Hill Gate,
above a sweet shop
in a triple-aspect sunny room.

That Evening

After you'd led me back along the Unthank Road,
past hedges and fences that no longer defined
ownership, simply displayed themselves
as one, uncanny whole,
      and after the name of the road seemed less
and less preposterous, yet so laden with meaning
one couldn't latch onto as if to resemble a turn
of phrase like *stumbling block*,
      and after you said that we'd got to go back
because you'd left a steak-and-kidney pudding on
the stove and I said nothing seemed the same anymore,
and you said nothing ever would seem the same
      (and I felt the bottom of my world cave-in like
I'd slipped down a well) – after all of that, with you
in the kitchen surrounded by steam, I went into our
room and sat down at my childhood piano:
      an object so familiar that I wanted to
hold it absolutely still while the carpet started
tilting and unfurling, and the curtains rolled in-and-
out-of-themselves with their zig-zaggy patterns.
      I looked at the black and white keys, thinking
these will only change if I touch them – if I play them,
my whole long relationship with sound might be
altered for ever.
      So I kept my hands still in my lap, moved
away to the sofa and closed both my eyes
and waited, and hoped it would stop.

The Woman Who Cries

by Pablo Picasso

It arrived in a clean white envelope
stamped Rotterdam,
as if he were trying to gain perspective.

I'd hoped for a neutral image –
a canal, a piece of Delft,
but the message read:

don't be *La Femme Qui Pleure* –
and underneath he'd underlined the title.

So I turned the card over and there she was:
fractured, pitiful, a red-and-blue lifeboat lodged
in her hair, driven mad by her own salt waters.

I kept her close to me for days
until I began to feel grateful,

grateful for knowing such a man,
a man who could match me to a painting
that summarised the trouble we were in.

Moving On

First there is the thing itself:
the going over and over it,
the trying-to-forget it,
the dreaming,
the re-wounding,
going over and over
again and again
the reminders.

Then the dampening down:
the getting how not-to-forget-it
because of the endless reminders,
due to the endless reminders,
the almost re-wounding
but more like forgetting for a moment,
a day, perhaps even a week
at least for a while.

Next the months in between:
when if you are lucky another thing happens,
equal to it in a way – terrible, but valuable –
rugged enough to submerse the original thing;
reminders dulled, dreams flattened
until a kind of fog sets in,
through which almost nothing
can be felt.

Then, by a miracle of love I guess,
the new thing starts to heal
and nothing seems able to re-kindle
the original event,
not even reminders that come and go,
year after year
until late one night
while you're driving through the dark
an unavoidable reminder of such unexpected
spark
        bursts in: not at all like dream –
pure emotional re-living
of the *actual* thing,
and all within the space of a hundred mile dash
down a fire-splashed highway
in a tear-storm of rage –
until finally, you realise
you are free.

Flowers from Mrs Yeats

by Winifred Nicholson

If I could only ever see one painting
please let it be this:

a distant wash of hills across the bay
stirred into sky, like custard

mixed with ice, tossed to a prism
then showered by wave upon wave

of light.

Two wavering croci guarding the loch,
each with its giant vase

pulsing deeper shades of green and blue,
as if her palette had been guided

by the great singers of the ancient world
whose voices were like pearls.

And the sea all brimming with watery life:
turquoise, sapphire, aquamarine

and the child-like seal with its sleek black coat
near the sand-stone bar

and the white.

Finishing the Peanuts

is the start of a sentence by Sylvia Plath
that somebody posted on Twitter.
Wonder how she'd feel about an extract
from her diary being used by a stranger
to wave at the world?

I've no idea;
finishing the peanuts sounds so complete,
like a finely knitted twinset
with a rise and falling rhythm to it
like a swallowing,
before its quiet journey forward to

we brought in a little paper bag. . .

how beautiful is that,
and when you put them together
finishing the peanuts we brought in a little paper bag. . .
god, that's beautiful.
I can almost sense the peanuts on my tongue;
small and darkly roasted, slightly greasy, slightly salt

or maybe plain with frilly outer skins
but maybe not;
maybe hidden softly in their shells.
Imagine Sylvia shelling nuts in Regents Park
or round the back of St Marks
where even now there's a slight grimy feeling

especially in October,
with the peacocks squawking
behind the sealed-off entrance to the zoo.
And then there's the *brought* –
did she mean they brought them with them
in the little paper bag?

getting out of a car? or maybe she meant
they finished the nuts while bringing them into
where –
perhaps she wrote 'bought'
and the person who copied it added an 'r'
does 'brought' mean 'bought' in American

I'd kind of like to know,
and also who exactly is the *we*
that brought them in that little paper bag,
or brought them into the place
which they may or may not have visited
or maybe lived in, was it she and Ted ?

It is probably sexist to bring Ted in at all,
to glamourise her with the addition of Ted
which she probably wouldn't have wanted,
or maybe she did,
depending on the state of their relationship
if this was their relationship.

What if the peanuts were still in their shells
where were *they* left?
inside the bag? I can't really see her screwing it up
and dropping it somewhere, or leaving it
for someone else to manage
inside the place they may, or may not have been

in the process of entering
I like to think they were hot little peanuts,
bought from a peanut seller somewhere cold and
quite rainy and of course I could look it up,
stop this small investigation like you can look
everything up, find any answer that you want.

There are so many questions that don't need
answering, don't need to be snapped-off,
finished by a quick Google search
that prevents all wondering, all imagining
because the next part of her sentence
is such a delight:

and the cellophane parcel of . . .

so: *finishing the peanuts we brought in a little paper bag*
and the cellophane parcel of . . .
perhaps it's because someone called me out once
for using the word cellophane that I so adore it here;
imagine the sound of a flashy little crinkly parcel
containing what? I love her surprise:

dried figs. . .

so: *finishing the peanuts we brought*
in a little paper bag
and the cellophane parcel of dried figs . . .
no need to find out what comes next.
Sylvia liked the word cellophane,
she ate peanuts from a little paper bag.

Letter from Lola

'Lola de Valence' by Edouard Manet

Paris, 1861

Sir,

Had you been told never to touch the oranges growing in
your mother's courtyard, long for sangria that can only
be made on days when tomatoes turn golden,
imagine a time when your father will bring home the shoes
that were measured for you on your fourteenth birthday

and now you are fifteen,

you might better understand what *waiting* means:
the shiver in my shawl, my famous skirt, my ribbons
– all these gave opportunity for movement, even my shadow.
Instead, you have fixed me,
standing alone in a reddening light, with a gaze

that is not of my making.

You, who have so frequently travelled to the Porte Dauphine,
watched me dazzle with my fan, undulate like a hawk,
stamp, bow, arch, quiver, hold the attention of a thousand eyes,
you render me thus?
The likeness has caused me much scandal

and to make matters worse

this poem by your friend Baudelaire in his libellous book
called *The Evil Flowers!*
Next week I face Paris again, dance Sardana, Fandango,
Flamenco, Bolero, even your favourite Muñeira.
I doubt you will search your heart

and wonder if it was worth it:

bring me no lilies, no champagne
none of your usual civilities.
I look forward to returning to my country,
especially to Madrid – a city whose galleries I believe
you would benefit from visiting.

A once fond admirer,

Lola de Valence
Prima Ballerina of the Troupe Campubri

Des Pas sur la Neige

Claude Debussy (triste et lente)

Tracks fan out
in what's left of the light,

sifting the paw-padded eiderdown lawn

where deer stopped still in the
dead of the night,

breathing out patterns

like wings lifting-off
into fog.

Vapour is turning to ice.

Powdery cabbages way-mark the places
where paths used to be.

No-one is risking the crystalline road.

Drifting is forecast.
Time slows to a grey beat.

Bodhisattva

6th century bronze figurine R.A.A. 'Bronze' exhibition.

Between Uma with her semi-precious stones
and Venus examining her toes
you sit pensive, exquisitely petite,
emanating peace.

A six inch goddess in the company
of life-size casts;
no veins, or individual muscle groups,
just the tilt of your head
toward the profile of your hand.
A gesture that leads me to consider
whether your fingertips were ever meant
to touch your chin.

I marvel at how you
hold your own
when giant Perseus is in the other room,
dangling the head of Medusa.

Weekend

She knew that at some point they would have to get undressed
but it wasn't clear when.

A paraglider had swept up from the beach.
He'd asked if she were feeling cold, if she'd like to go down.

She'd answered *yes*, reached for the zip of her anorak.
He'd put his arm around her.

On the way back they stopped at some shops.
He helped her through with the bags
before flopping down on the sofa like he'd said he would.

She stood there watching as two bags of shopping
relaxed on his kitchen floor:
there lay the kidneys in their plastic wrappers,

the sausages too big to fit the frying pan,
the tomatoes, the mushrooms, his small tin of peas,
the steak that would have to be bashed

while he flicks through the Radio Times
which he'd told her he often likes to do on a Sunday
afternoon as it reminds him of his parents' place.

She'd remembered to reverse into the drive,
but had decided to ignore his advice
about the magnolia tree.

She can see her car now, through the kitchen window,
covered in dark, waxy leaves.

Tax Return

Yes, I have tried to use a password
without a user ID,
several times, like an elderly ape exploring
the use of a primitive tool:

typing it in, leaving the other box empty;
tapping, typing, leaving, typing –
persisting – just like Sally and Jonathan
must have done for the person

who took their photographs
for this leaflet entitled; *'Slim and Trim
in 28 Days'* which I should not be
reading at the moment.

Yes, it explains how to do a *'Squat Jump'.*
They probably felt a sense of unease that
after all their success, it had come to this
and yes, it is my fault. Everyone knows

to keep user ID's and passwords together
in secretive places, like Sally and Jonathan
probably do, though Sally and Jonathan
more likely have someone to do all this

for them – they wouldn't sit whimpering
over a tax return at two in the morning,
wondering why they are poor when they
had all the advantages the 20th century

could possibly offer, and now they can't
even complain because so many young
people are heading towards far worse
situations, like competing with robots:

yes, imagine that –
imagine having to compete with a robot
when all you want to do
is fall in love.

A Softness

Lifted by an eiderdown
while someone snips the ties that hold you down
is a way of trying to say it.

Another way,
when swoon is not a word you want to use
or drowsiness, or bloom, is maybe float –

float towards her
mid-air, half dying on the wing
towards a tumbling,

breathy sound.

A Few Small Deceits

1 parking ticket
6 pints of milk
3 visits to a friend who lives in the same direction
the suggestion of a last-minute holiday
because going away on your own can be helpful for those
who feel their life is meaningless
a new screen that closes super-quick
2 pings that didn't mean the bank had left a message
a kiss that never happened
1 sudden departure from a living room
numerous hugs that no-one prevented
the need to keep upright on a sloping hill
(so we had to hold hands)
1 photo of a double rainbow (without human shadows)
1 photo of a single rainbow (without human shadows)
5 quietly prepared meals to suggest domestic harmony
14 episodes of calm washing up that should have been done
by somebody else
1 visit to a town centre to buy walking boots
as if this town doesn't sell them
a visual migraine attack

After Yesterday

whenever I try to form sensible thoughts
slow down   back away
my body seeks yours
as if tuned to a perfect union
with you

we've barely met

I know very little about how these things go
in the real world
try to imagine
the ways we might be with one another
my body seeks yours

I have tuned to you

these thoughts of perfection leave me feeling nervous
it isn't about that I say to myself
yet it is
there's a long way to go before easiness
which I try not to think must be part of this attraction

we made a decision

I no longer know what it is
ask myself how this can possibly go wrong
when love has taken charge of the arrangements
as if I'd never read a story in my life
never seen a movie

How the Watchmaker Talks to Herself

Take the trans-axial with its micro-epicyclic gears,
high-precision lunar train, bevelled wheels,
transparent sapphire wheels which could have been
useful for pin-pointing the exact moment
when you showed me how to kiss

as if a smaller, lighter spring
had avoided its escapement while we stood by that door,
without the need for pivots, stepped into a carriage
that hadn't cancelled out its poise errors.

Now all I can hear is that song,
the one that Francoise Hardy used to sing about the door
closing, the car driving away, and the tourbillon?
It would have had to be still: cage stationary
until we stopped for breath,

held each other closer, leaned against the frame of the door
to steady ourselves
while the seconds caught up with their minutes
and I wondered how your skin would feel.

Why must this spring be re-wound every second.
I want to get back to the moment when *don't go*
breaking my heart must have passed through your mind
– as for this tiny little lunar train what can I say?

such a train as is made for lunatics like us
who can't get on can't get off, don't understand
how to jump the dead seconds, calibrate the simplest
form of revolution – and the days they are ticking,
the hours they are turning to stone.

Astonishing Sonatas

When she stepped in through my front door
I felt as if she'd moved the floor
beneath my desk, and opened up the piano lid
and let the light come flooding in.

She hardly missed a beat that day,
not even when we tried to play
those astonishing sonatas
by Poulenc. I hope we die of laughter

in a car or on a bike;
me riding pillion, her like a stranger
only not – white hot – brimming with life
and gorgeous ideas, and fizz

with a capital F though she left
just as soon as she came,
ran off somewhere distant in the rain
beyond my house, beyond my lane.

This Rush of Love

is almost more than I can take
the absolute delight of you
in every single way and numerous
ways you feel how much I feel
you know already how I feel
how we two feel
inside this rush of welcome love
and yes it's like a dream
and not a dream we feel the same
it seems we feel the same
the absolute delight
of knowing one another
of touching the slightest part of you
please   bring it on
bring more and more
until I almost die from love
and save myself for you and me
for me and you I curl
I curl into the thought of you.

Garden

let the river take you
>to a place of understanding

the garden is within

you cannot know where or how
>you will enter

there may or may not be a rainbow

wild with grasses and blustery showers
>you will soon lose your way

let the river take you all the same

to her softness
>to the warmth of her skin

Zephyr

There were so many different types of leaves
with which to dance
while autumn was being discussed;

half lines up-ended, verbs flitting away
as if poetry were shedding a skin.

The colour of her sky sickened for a physical dictionary.

Certain poems demand it
like the one she'd been trying to write for a while
called 'Zephyr'

by which she might topple her overflowing dustbin
of ideas, sweep apathy away,

experiment with stillness while the world goes mad.

A pointless thing to do, people tried to say
while she tried imagining a ruffling;

the effect it might have on this soddening power.

There was melancholy to consider –
not plain old melancholy[1] – the type she used to feel
in the days before all of this started.

---

[1] 'plain old melancholy' comes from the poem *Saffron* by
Paul Muldoon

Not Forgetting

a week in which forty nine people were gunned in a club, fifty others wounded and god knows how many more traumatically injured and our hearts went out to them we said, and our hearts did go out to them, and our minds didn't want to but soon were imagining trying to stop a two year old being snatched by a gator – Alligator Seizes Disney World Boy – but let's get this straight: nothing can seize a 'Disney World Boy' this was a child at the edge of a lagoon; paddling and falling, rising and squealing with delight as his mom held his hand to steady him and we felt so bad trying not to imagine being trapped in that bar with the guy who wanted to kill all those men, because they need remembering too and now on this bus, right now, another boy, because I'm telling you this is not a man, is shouting to his phone that he wants to kill his brother and nobody knows how close he'd been to it this afternoon – if he'd had something with him he'd have done it right then and there – then and there he'd have done it if he'd had something with him and I feel like putting my arms around this boy but I can't.

Cemetery

We knew about the cemetery,
four hundred yards on the left
and we'd discussed it;

people die all the time
so they might as well be buried there

though late at night, when we were lying still
on our deep-filled mattress
in the quiet,

I couldn't help imagining
how close we all were

and remembering how,
weeks before my mother's death,
she justified it by saying she didn't envy me

living on, into the twenty first century,
with all that was likely to happen.

Watching these clouds,
and the wood pigeon's flight to the uppermost
twig of the tall poplar tree,

and this light that persists,
I have decided never to use such an argument.

Two Gorillas

Hands behind backs, feet slightly apart,
they concentrate on human imitation,
intently observe the expressions of their keepers
who seem worried
and tired,
as if this strange form of parenting
may never end.

One gorilla has a paunch,
the other is slimmer.

There they stand, upright on their legs,
watching the men
who've looked after them for years;
the years since their mothers were poached
by other men
who didn't give a fuck.

Better to behave like these men
– though it was men who tore their mothers
from them –
than risk an escape to the forest
where perhaps they would have to pretend
they had never left.

There's a Certain Type of Driving

listening to the frantic frantic news
if you're able to bear all the physical forces
of nature –
your stomach your stomach so very confused
by the time
and no sustenance
confusing the lining   when to digest all the spicy stuff
they'd serve you on these non-stop flights
that they're telling you about
New York to Sydney they'd need you awake
while you'd dream you were asleep
awake when they'd want you to sleep
asleep when I thought I was awake
and ahead of myself by the five bar gate
an early morning squirrel
just starting to leap
to dance across the tarmac
o tell it tell it   stay right there
god I see it understand start   turn   start to run back
thwack its tiny body goes   thwack
beneath me as the news carries on about the protest
all the protest going on
how I saw it understand   start   turn   start to run back
but for the shadow of my chassis
didn't fix it   couldn't tell it   stay right there
not dance across the tarmac
asleep when I thought I was awake
awake when they'd want you to wake and they'd keep you
awake on those non-stop flights
with your stomach your stomach so very confused
by the time
and no sustenance confusing the lining.

Killer Whale

on watching 'Blackfish' by Gabriela Cowperthwaite

I'd switched on out of nothing better to do.
Soon I am watching a boy in a wet suit,
tugged by his foot by a black and white whale

then plunged at speed
to the bottom of the SeaWorld lagoon,
because that's where this is happening – Florida.

His lungs are about to burst.
Next it's the turn of the trainee attendant
who's run out of fish;

she hasn't blown her whistle quite right,
the orca doesn't like it so she gets dragged under,
tossed in the air and savaged.

Then somebody asks the obvious question:
why do they keep him?
Next they show him lying still in the practice pool;

fin flipped over, motionless,
his lonely penis being milked for its sperm
and the trainers explain how they need it

to keep the whole operation going, but someone
points out they are breeding psychopaths
and I think why on *earth* am I watching this?

Later that week I dream I'm a bear,
completely protected in thick brown fur,
at ease with myself in the wild.

So Now

I must decide whether to put this piece of shrink-wrap
paper in the re-cycle bin,

can I be bothered to find out whether it really should go in there?
can I be bothered to take this piss-little decision seriously

in the privacy of my kitchen, where, whenever I notice
anything, I realise I have sinned,

that I am part of the Endless Destruction,
part of the reason why things have gone so terribly wrong
and I shouldn't be eating meat, and I shouldn't be

driving my car, and I shouldn't be going to Paris next week
on a plane, I should be taking the train
which will cost me far, far more.

All I can think about is why I haven't lost any weight
this week. Can't even be bothered to find out about

the virus: o come let it get me, let it get me soon
before it morphs into something far, far worse.

Yesterday, the man who came to clear the drain told me
about a 'little mouse' he'd noticed near the man-hole cover

and writing this nasty little poem is making me feel even
worse, so much worse than writing a successful, big

important poem that might just be included
in an actual poetry magazine.

2084

A woman thought she saw a bush
through something called binoculars.

We know not to ask its location
due to the crumbling of ravines.

More rains are expected.

Some say rains come
not through the movement of rock
but through some other means
we were taught to forget.

The apple pip is still in its plastic bag,
as transparent as the year they sealed it

and a new planet's been identified,
orbiting a sun,
with optimum conditions
for biological life.

We do not ask about its distance
from Earth.

There are ruins you can visit.

Lemons

I don't know where you started out
but you're so welcome to remain here

in my bowl on this table
in this temporary place,

nestled in amongst these English apples
like the best of friends.

Beyond the window three plump sheep,
a blackbird calls its afternoon sleep-well

as if it cares about you, or me,
what goes on in this dead-end little street.

There's the mini-bottle from last night
with its optimistic label – *Vino Spumante*

Italia – I shall fill it with water,
go pick a sprig of winter Hellebore,

place it like a little palm
to remind you of home.

ACKNOWLEDGEMENTS

The following poems first appeared in:
The Poetry Review (2020): *Sea Creature Regrows Entire Body*
and *Thursday*
Ledbury Poetry Festival (2020) Lockdown Poems: *Draft Email*
The New European: *Stupor* (2018) and *Lemons* (2019)
Ambit Magazine (2018): *Green Suitcase*
The North: (2018): *Weekend*
Live Canon Anthology (2016): *Cemetery*
'Faber New Poets 13' (2016) *Rehearsal for a Night-time Scene with Thunder, A Mess of Strangers, Norfolk Winter '72, The Woman who Cries,* and *Killer Whale*

WITH THANKS TO:

Stuart Bartholomew, Gill Barr, Sinéad Morrissey, Greta Stoddart, Annie Freud, Matthew Hollis, Sarah Steele, Sarah Fisher, Gladstone's Library and The Arts Council England for their encouragement, guidance and support.

ABOUT THE AUTHOR:

Elaine Beckett's debut pamphlet *Faber New Poets 13* was published by Faber & Faber in 2016. Her work has appeared in *The Poetry Review, Ambit, The North, The New European* and in numerous anthologies. In 2018 she received a Veronica Powles Memorial Scholarship from Gladstone's Library. In 2020 she was shortlisted for the Bridport Prize and longlisted for the National Poetry Competition. She has appeared on Radio 3's *The Verb*.

Elaine grew up in Kent and studied music, film and architecture in London. She studied piano and composition at the Guildhall School of Music and Drama, then trained as a music therapist. She worked for many years as a university lecturer and holds a PhD from the University of York. She is a graduate of the National Film and TV School and has composed for theatre and TV. Elaine holds a degree in Architecture from UCL and currently supervises arts therapists working in the UK and abroad.

ABOUT VERVE POETRY PRESS

Verve Poetry Press is a quite new and already award-winning press that focused initially on meeting a local need in Birmingham - a need for the vibrant poetry scene here in Brum to find a way to present itself to the poetry world via publication. Co-founded by Stuart Bartholomew and Amerah Saleh, it now publishes poets from all corners of the UK - poets that speak to the city's varied and energetic qualities and will contribute to its many poetic stories.

Added to this is a colourful pamphlet series, many featuring poets who have performed at our sister festival - and a poetry show series which captures the magic of longer poetry performance pieces by festival alumni such as Polarbear, Matt Abbott and Geraldine Carver.

In 2019 the press was voted Most Innovative Publisher at the Saboteur Awards, and won the Publisher's Award for Poetry Pamphlets at the Michael Marks Awards.

Like the festival, we strive to think about poetry in inclusive ways and embrace the multiplicity of approaches towards this glorious art.

www.vervepoetrypress.com
@VervePoetryPres
mail@vervepoetrypress.com